Unafraid
standing up to the bully of fear

Holly Sue Ruddock

Copyright © 2020 Holly Sue Ruddock

All rights reserved.

ISBN: 9798605243861

Acknowledgement

How does one write about being unafraid without recognizing the ones who put their lives on the line for our freedom?

This little book is dedicated to my incredibly brave, warrior children and their spouses. Cody and Whitney, Ryley, Sydney and Kyle, and Jessey.

Your fearless service to our country and life of sacrifice for our freedom has challenged me to live bold and courageous.

You are all my heroes!

"Evil is powerless if the good are unafraid"
-Ronald Reagan

Preface

This booklet was written with the intention of being a quick read to combat the fears many of us face.

If you're like me, you need something that can get you to the meat of the message. I love a good book, but sometimes I am so desperate to tackle the situation at hand, and don't have the energy to spend on the build-up to the story. I need to get to the center of the tootsie pop with the one-two-three "crunch"!

In writing this, I reference to stories in the Bible that most of us know. If you are unfamiliar with them, then I encourage you to refresh yourself, get acquainted with the struggles these men and women faced and how they became overcomer's.

I pray you hear my heart. I pray you hear what Jesus is saying and can apply what the Holy Spirit reveals with the Heavenly Strategies He imparts.

If you could hear me, you would hear me cheering you on: Be brave! Don't back down! Hold your ground! Your due season is here!

Disclaimer: An apprehension of creepy crawly, eight legged devils, or any bug for that matter, is wisdom and I will not judge you.

Storms

"The devil whispered, 'You can't withstand the storm!' And I replied, 'I AM the storm!'" - Unknown

I love this quote! It's such a declaration of faith and fearlessness. If you relate to this quote, it means you have faced a typhoon that felt as if it was from hell itself.

Usually, *storms* like these are sent to distract, discourage, destroy, and to downtrodden us. They are commissioned to make us tremble in fear, rethink our excursion, reevaluate our adventure, and eventually, retreat. We tuck our tails and throw a blankey over our heads and hide.

There are those storms that are exciting. They can be beautiful and refreshing. Who doesn't love a good thunderstorm in the summer or the pelting rain on a cold fall night? It's practically magic.

And then there are those storms that turn dangerous and destructive, and the splendor of the storm is replaced with white-knuckled-hang-on-for-your-life-God-get-me-out-of-here fear. The lightning crashes just a little too close to home. The wind is whipping more than your hair back and forth.

Being fearless in these *life* down-pours, isn't always about feeling brave, it's more about doing things with our knees knocking until we fear less and less. It's about taking the looming risk of failure, raising our sails, and facing the crashing waves with a giant presence of faith.

Facing a hell-sent storm is confronting a bully that has been sent to make your life miserable. Fear is the "playground" bully. But it's not lunch money he is taking, it's our peace, our confidence, our joy, our purpose, and our dignity.

In these few pages we WILL confront the bullies that try to reduce us to nervous little schoolgirls, shaking in our knee-highs.

We will discuss a few areas we must learn to be unafraid in:

- A Destiny Stopping Storm
- Grief
- Depression
- Insecurities
- The Pause

The difference between a natural fear and a spirit of fear, is the spirit of fear comes with torment. Torment is void of all hope or joy. It is filled with only despair, pain, trauma, or anguish.

The web dictionary describes torment as a severe physical or mental suffering. What I found really interesting; is it was described as a noun. This torment *thing* is a monster!

*"There is no fear in love [**dread does not exist**], but full-grown (complete, **perfect) love turns fear out of doors and expels every trace of terror**! For fear brings with it the thought of punishment(torment), and [so] he who is afraid has not reached the full maturity of love [is not yet grown into love's complete perfection]." 1 John 4:18 Amplified*

Here's an interesting fact to ponder: the root word of *torment* comes from that of clipping a bird's wings; making them flightless. What a vivid description. Fear makes us afraid to take the risk, the leap, the jump of faith. It takes away our ability to dream, hope, aspire and **soar**.

When I think of a flightless bird, I think of a chicken; the very animal that represents being afraid. (Anyone thinking of the movie Back to the Future? "Nobody calls me chicken")

The plan of the enemy is to not only make us flightless, it's to frighten us out of ever trying to fly; to remove all hope to ever soar again. An eagle whose wings are clipped is a prisoner. They might as well be at Foster Farms.

"And you did not receive the 'spirit of religious duty,' leading you back into the fear of never being good enough. But you have received the 'Spirit of full acceptance,' enfolding you into the family of God. And you will never feel orphaned, for as he rises up within us, our spirits join him in saying the words of tender affection, 'Beloved Father!'"
Romans 8:15 The Passion Bible

I can remember a few times in my life when the spirit of fear bullied me to the point of being tormented. One particular time of being oppressed by fear was when we had our two oldest boys deployed at the same time.

My nights were filled with sleeplessness, anxious thoughts, pleading prayers and my days were petitions of safety for my deployed boys.

I had to guard my peace in those uncertain times. I had to avoid the news, a few people, and social media posts that could instill fear and dread.

I could physically feel my body fight the oppression of fear. My shoulders were sore, and my body ached from carrying the weight of my worry. I felt small and my prayers felt weak. It was new territory for me, and I had to find my way through this unfamiliar ground.

And though I knew God was big enough for all the unknowns, *and* I knew He was watching over our children; I also knew bad things did happen to good, godly people who put their trust in the Lord and that we were not immune to trouble.

I knew faith wasn't about believing awful things would never happen. No, faith was about believing in God's goodness and sovereignty when trouble came. It was hoping in Him, anchoring in Him, hiding in Him. Crawling as close as I possibly could to Him in my stormy days.

I was being tossed around by a storm of what-ifs and worry waves. It took every ounce of strength to get up in the morning and face another day. But every new day Jesus would help me muster up enough strength to put my armor on, fluff out my tutu, and charge at another 24 hours; one minute at time.

On occasions, my war cry was more of a whimper; a prayer to not falter and to not succumb to fearful "what-ifs" that loomed in my head. I had to *faith* my faith. I was frightened of the possible "what-ifs".

What if my boys were injured, went missing, or were killed?

And then, one day one of my "what-ifs" turned into a reality when my middle son was injured and medically evacuated out of Afghanistan.

Ryley suffered an extreme head trauma, leaving him with seizures, memory loss, and personality change. What I had feared had come upon me.

In those days of troubles and heartache, fear pounded and kicked at my door in a ferocious rage, and in my surprise, a supernatural faith began to rise up within me.

As a family we had to navigate unknown waters; dark seas and toppling waves. Ryley had to heal, re-learn certain life skills, and grieve pieces of his life that were permanently changed.

That scary day, I faced that "what if" with an "even if" and my mustard seed faith sprouted like a chia pet. I actually felt my hope grow stronger and my faith more aggressive, *after* Ryley was injured.

It's been a few years since Ry's injury, and we have sailed across quite a few stormy seas for his care, his benefits, and his independence. But the courage Jesus gave me the day Ryley was wounded has only grown fiercer, deeper, and more trusting.

We may need to voyage a hurricane every now and then, but I have leaned into the faithfulness of Jesus and the "even ifs". I do it trembling, and I do it trusting. It's not all sunny days, but it is days filled with the Son.

Storms similar to these have a way of filtering us; removing the debris of unbelief, doubt, pride and our own agendas- drawing out *The Woman of Courage*.

She was there all along, but sunny days don't reveal the warrior.

When our war cry is a whimper and our knees are knocking, we saddle up anyway and face the typhoon that is heading our way.

A woman of faith, even in fear, has an instinct that takes over because **she is wired to run towards trouble, not away from it**, regardless of the "what ifs".

But with that determination, we still have to jump the waves of fear, feelings of defeat, and deep heartache.

You can't be brave if you're not facing a storm that terrifies you.

"But my righteous one will live by faith. And I take no pleasure in the one who shrinks back." But we do not belong to those who shrink back and are

destroyed, but to those who have faith and are saved. Hebrews 10:38-39

The Greek meaning of shrink back is to be cowardly, or to stealthily retreat. I picture somebody walking into conflict and before anybody sees them, they quietly back up and secretly slide out of the room unnoticed.

But we will not cower to the bully, we will stand up to him. If I were to describe a bully it would be this: someone who makes you feel powerless or enslaved. The emotion of dread that comes with the knowledge of just having to face them, can cause physical sickness.

I was bullied a few times in my life; when I was child and in my adult years as well. The oppression that harasses and strips you of dignity is crippling. But then something rockets inside of you that says, "Enough!"

When I was about five or six years old I was bullied relentlessly by a neighbor girl. The sad thing is, I considered her my best friend. She was horrible to me and I was happy to let her be, just so I had a friend to play with.

Until one day my dad told me that if I continued to let Kari beat me up, he was going to give me a whoopin. Well, that was all I needed to hear.

The very next day I went looking for a fight. I picked, I poked, and I prodded at the bear until she was ready to brawl. I took all my past years of being bullied (all three or four of them) and channeled them into one marvelous punch.

She went home crying, and I went back to playing; with this huge satisfaction that I had just settled the score.

However, the thing about a bully is they always seem to know other tormentors who they can rally to come fight their cause with them. Gangs. Mobs. Mafias. Isn't that just like the enemy?

You have a great victory, an incredible breakthrough or promotion, and that blasted devil comes at you with an arsenal of weapons he had stashed away. He rallied the troops and the ants came marching.

Don't panic! This is his last-ditch effort to clip the eagle wings and turn her into a chicken. This is what my so called "best friend" did; she went home and gathered her posse, which were her older brothers, and they cornered me when I was walking to another girlfriend's house.

They beat the stuffing out of me. When I made it to my girlfriend Cheryl's house her mom saw me all disheveled and called my dad. I sat in Cheryl's living room doing my gasping cry. Then I heard my dad coming in his giant, gas guzzling 1970 something, station wagon; tires squealing, and pedal throttled. **My father came to my rescue!**

But I wasn't consoled at that moment. He was too angry; but not at me. I followed him to the car and got in, all while doing the ugly throw-up-cry.

He flew around the block and parked directly in front of Kari's house. But he wasn't there for my "bestie", he was there to confront the father of the bully.

My dad stood in the doorway and called out Kari's dad, but the old guy was too drunk to fight and too afraid to get out of his chair. I can still see to this day, my courageous father standing in the doorway yelling at Rob to get up and settle this. But the man was afraid of my dad, and Rob never got out of his recliner. That was the last time I ever had to fight my childhood bully.

Think about this: your Heavenly Father is teaching you to stand up to the enemy on a daily basis. He is teaching you to not shrink back or cower.

You will feel fear facing your bully, but The Father of Heaven and Earth is well equipped to confront the father of lies. And although He will not threaten you with a whoopin, He is saying "Stand up child. Do not fear. Be courageous. Set your face like flint. Hold your ground and face your giant."

God has got your back. And when it looks like the enemy has just whooped ya good, Abba Father is quick to get in his chariot station wagon and scoop you up. And then the fun starts. He calls out the enemy for the harassment of His daughter. And that coward will not get out of his lazy boy because he fears your papa and knows your daddy means business.

Don't Shrink back, sisters. Instead, get to know Papa God and how much He loves you. You are worth the screeching of tires to come to the rescue.

The enemy's tactic is to get us to wither away by cornering us with torment, trauma, or trials. He works double shifts with the intent to get us overwhelmed with burdens, anxiety, and worry. He corners us as he stirs up trouble that causes storms that *appear* to have no way of escape.

Hurricanes rage and we must sail through them. Some of us put ourselves in these stormy moments, but most storms we face are caused by a catastrophic event that takes us by surprise. A typhoon caused, not by our choosing or doing, but by life's cruel hand. Or in some cases, the domino effect from another persons' decision: the tsunami of a loved one passing away, financial ruin, a health crisis or chronic illness of you or someone you love. Perhaps it's a cyclone of your spouse's moral failures, or of your own past mistakes that haunt you. There's a childhood trauma, a drug-addict child, a failed marriage, or even caregiving for someone you love; storms you can't escape from. You must cross the wild waters.

We see all the possible things that can, and do, go wrong in a storm. We see the ravages of harsh winds and the aftermath of a squall. **Life events, or other people's choices, become *our* mess to clean up or *our* bully to confront.**

It's unfair, I know. But keep in mind, even if our boat sinks, Jesus walks on water. **He is not detoured by catastrophic events. It's where miracles come thundering out of!**

*"He saw that they were in serious trouble, rowing hard and struggling against the wind and waves. About three o'clock in the morning Jesus came toward them, walking on the water. He intended to go past them, but when they saw him walking on the water, they cried out in terror, thinking he was a ghost. They were all terrified when they saw him. But Jesus spoke to them at once. "**Don't be afraid**," he said. "**Take courage! I am here!** " Then he climbed into the boat, and the wind stopped. They were totally amazed,"*
Mark 6:48-51 NLT

In this day-to-day thing we call *existence*, we get up-close and personal with a whole lotta crud. Blow after blow, trial after trial, and disappointment after disappointment. We begin to feel ourselves shrinking, eroding away with the rushing water.

We feel like we are being boiled and quickly evaporating away into the air, until we are only a wisp of a person. We are rowing hard and struggling against the waves and then suddenly, we see Him. He sees us and then He says to you, "Take courage daughter, I am here." And the winds stop.

THE DESTINY STOPPING STORM

"Courage is being scared to death but saddling up anyway"- John Wayne

In Mark 4 the disciples start out full of faith: seeing miracles Jesus performed, sweet moments spent with their Master, teaching them of the secrets of heaven, explaining the mysteries of the parables and a faith being tested.

Parables like the farmers sowing seeds, or the story of the lamp and making sure not to put our light under a basket but let our light shine where all could see.

And my personal favorite; the parable of faith like a mustard seed. Jesus was building some groundwork with the parables of faith being tested, because a storm was about to come.

These faith parables are both challenging and encouraging, and they were the ones the disciples heard *before* a raging storm. Mark 4:35-41 explains "The rest of the story".

As evening came, Jesus said to his disciples, "Let's cross to the other side of the lake." So they took Jesus in the boat and started out, leaving the crowds behind (although other boats followed). But soon a fierce storm came up. High waves were breaking into the boat, and it began to fill with water. Jesus was sleeping at the back of the boat with his head on a cushion. The disciples woke him up, shouting, "Teacher, don't you care that we're going to drown?" When Jesus woke up, he rebuked the wind and said to the waves, "Silence! Be still!" Suddenly the wind stopped, and there was a great calm. Then he asked them, "Why are you afraid? Do you still have no faith?" The disciples were absolutely terrified. "Who is this man?" they asked each other. "Even the wind and waves obey him!"
Mark 4:35-41 NLT

Let's imagine we are the disciples and Jesus says to us, "load up in the boat, I need to go to the other side." We leave the crowd behind. A crowd that was hungry and receptive. A crowd that loved us and viewed us as special. A crowd we have ministered to and poured our lives out on. We leave them to cross a sea that we have no idea what is waiting on the other side.

Jesus wants us to follow Him into an unknown place. We look up to the sky, the clouds look dark, it's obvious the weather is changing. At first the crowd wants to follow Jesus, but the waves begin to get a little rough, and the crowd thinks, "never mind, I've got the fullness of God. I'll just make my way back to land where it's safe." And so the masses fall back.

But we're the ones in the boat with Jesus. We can't go back, we're committed. But there's nothing to fear, everything will be fine. Jesus is with us and He is perfectly relaxed.

The waves lull Him to sleep. He grabs one of those life preservers that looks like a donut and He takes a siesta. Then the waves get bigger and we want to hang on to the life saver Jesus is using as a pillow!

The winds get harsher and begin to tear at our sails. The wind stings our skin and violently tosses us around. We might even lose our lunch. But we've been in storms before and we've got this. Like Peter and his brothers; they knew storms, they've fished in worse.

And then the water becomes merciless, the gales savage. It's almost like some evil force was trying to *keep us* from the other side. Waves of torment grip our hearts, and without thinking, we panic and blame Jesus.

"Don't you even care?" we cry. "We're drowning here!" we yell.

Jesus wakes up; stretches, yawns, pops His stiff neck caused by that stupid "pillow" we wanted. I imagine He even pours himself a cup of coffee from a thermos.

When He's finally finished with his post-nap routine, His thunderous voice booms at the storm, "SILENCE! BE STILL!" And a great calm falls over the seas.

We want to feel peace, we need to feel it, but somehow we only feel remorse. And with one look, Jesus cuts right to our hearts, not to shame us but to question us, "Why are you afraid? Do you still have no faith?"

We quietly sit down and remember the sower's story and the seed of faith that was tested. We remember the parable of our lamps oil, and our lamps just got doused with sea water. And what about our tiny little mustard seed faith? Well, it drowned.

However, this storm was just the beginning of the victories and miracles to come. Jesus needed His disciples to get over their fear of storms and grow faith *big* in their spirits, for they were about step out onto new territory.

They now knew a little bit more about this Jesus guy they followed. They got up-close and personal with the Master of the storms. They experienced a new level of power and authority. Even the winds and waves obeyed Him.

Mark 5:1-20 tells us what happens when Jesus gets to the other side of the water. It describes a tragic story of a tormented soul, left alone, ensnared and bullied by the enemy, shackled by man and abandon to live a life among the dead in a graveyard.

When Jesus climbed out of the boat, a man possessed by an evil spirit came out from the tombs to meet him. This man lived in the burial caves and could no longer be restrained, even with a chain. Whenever he was put into chains and shackles – as he often was – he snapped the chains from his wrists and smashed the shackles. No one was strong enough to subdue him. Day and night he wandered among the burial caves and in the hills, howling and cutting himself with sharp stones. Mark 5:2-5 NLT

Troubled doesn't even begin to explain the anguish this poor soul lived with. He ran wild, naked, and utterly destitute.

But then, one day, the shattered and broken man looks up from the tomb he was weathering a surprise storm in, and sees a boat coming. He squints his eyes. Even with a troubled mind and tormented spirit, he sees hope crossing a wild sea to get to him!

When Jesus was still some distance away, the man saw him, ran to meet him, and bowed low before him. Mark 5:6 NLT

Covered in nothing but dirt, scabs, bugs, and other things we won't mention, his eyes lock eyes with Jesus. Jesus *sees* him. He really sees him.

Jesus hops out of the boat with His eyes still fixed on the man that he just endured a hurricane to come see.

The pitiful, suffering fellow, consumed by the 2000 demons, runs towards the Redeemer, and get this; it's not the man that speaks first, it's the demons that beg for mercy. I can't imagine the torment this wretched soul lived in.

With a shriek, he screamed, "Why are you interfering with me, Jesus, Son of the Most High God? In the name of God, I beg you, don't torture me! Mark 5:7 NLT

I've only seen and experienced a demon possessed woman once in my life. We were on a mission trip and the victory she experienced after we prayed was miraculous. It was like she woke up from a walking sleep. She was actually mute, and her eyes were half open. But when she was delivered, she came alive and was a chatty chatterson, full of joy and excitement. It was miraculous and amazing

This man's desperate need for deliverance pulled Jesus and his disciples through a violent hurricane and raging sea. And Jesus, doing what He set out to do, sets the man free. He yanks 2000 demonic spirits out of the guy, like He pulled a molar, and then tosses those hideous lizards into a few pigs.

Spoiler alert, the demon possessed pigs jump into the sea that Jesus just weathered to get to the man. I don't know why that amuses me. But if satan sent a storm to stop Jesus from getting to the man, then why not let the waves that tried to destroy the mission, drench the ones who caused the storm?

And for the first time in years, the man sits, clothed, calm and at perfect peace. If you have ever, EVER experienced any type of torment in your life, then you might have a fraction of understanding as to what this *peace* feels like.

I could hang out on this bit of the story for hours. All the rage of the storm. All the fear. All the waves. All the gulps of water. All the gritted teeth and white knuckling grip. All the panic. And all the frustration the disciples had against Jesus for taking them through the hellacious storm was for this moment right here; this beautiful, precious pocket of peace.

The man understands what Jesus just crossed for him and what the disciples endured, and he is beyond grateful. His heart is lunged toward the One who harnessed a storm for *him*. Now he wants to get in the boat with Jesus and go to the other side of the waters with the storm walker.

How ironic. This guy knows what a storm is, he knows what it is to be bullied by a downpour of torment. But he thinks, "what's a violent windstorm after being terrorized by 2000 demons?"

You know the story; Jesus tells him "no" and instead makes him a missionary to the community nearby; to be a testament of the great things God has done. This miraculous deliverance is because someone, or a few *someone's*, were willing to stand up and endure a fear gripping, flesh shredding, knee knocking storm for another's victory

When we are *unafraid*, we walk into what would be a terrifying place and we terrify the enemy. We brave a storm to cast out demons, in Jesus' name, and then we sit with the once troubled and tormented and celebrate with them; a great and mighty victory.

They are smiling, clothed and calm, saturated in a peace that is beyond all understanding. And their peace and authentic joy was worth the few big gulps of water you took in while crossing the troubled seas.

Being unafraid means saying "YES" to Jesus when your insides are screaming "RUN AWAY".

For the past few years, I have been journeying through a health crisis and I have experienced the physical part of torment in my body. In August 2015 I had an emergency appendectomy with a bowel resection, the removal of a gut full of scar tissue and the scraping of severe adhesions, and I got to spend eight luxurious nights in the hospital. But hey, it was a great diet plan.

I was septic, and later would go septic two more times. The pain that came with this kind of infection and recovery was the closest I would say to torture. There was no relief. I wanted to die and felt like I was going to. In fact, I was giving Joe the passwords to all of our accounts to pay the bills (that may have scared him a bit).

I would feel the pain of the infection rising and knew I was becoming septic again. Utter panic would rise in me. I was tormented by the first sign of pain because I knew the impending torture that was to follow and, there was no way of escaping what I was about to endure.

I would beg God to stop the pain, but the agony only increased. It was the first time in my life I was in a desperate state of need. My husband was my nurse and my knight. He was a knight nurse. Joe would help me with the smallest of tasks: getting me dressed, showering, brushing my hair, and pray, pray, pray over me.

My Mom and her husband came and stayed with us so Joe could go back to work, while I stayed in bed and grew a rat's nest on the back of my head. If I wasn't in bed, then I was bowing to the thunder bucket, and if I wasn't throwing up, then I was hovering over a bowl with depilating nausea. I was a hot mess.

It was during another bout with sepsis, that my son, Cody, and his wife, Whitney, were up visiting. Cody sat by my bed and prayed in tongues while I cried and writhed in agony. During his prayer, I could feel peace wash over me, and I slept as the pain was reduced to waves. Cody then said to me, "you warred over me momma, it's my turn to war over you."

In my anguish and physical weakness, and thoughts of "God, just take me now", filling my mind; my son was pulling heaven down to earth and fighting a battle I had no strength to combat.

I was eventually hauled off in an ambulance and given an IV of pain meds and a second batch of high potent penicillin (this, by the way, was my second visit to the ER that day. Good times…)

But I will tell you, hearing my boy pray over me like he did, was almost worth that torment. I was on an island, suffering, and somebody was willing to confront the enemy on my behalf.

My sickness and survival required others to set aside their comfort, their time, and their funds, to invest in me. My husband suffered along with me. He felt helpless because he couldn't stop the suffering, he could only try to comfort it. My family rallied around me. My sister sent me essential oils of vast supply, which Joe likes to call "That Voodoo Stuff".

I usually can muster the strength to push on and pull out some sort of fight. I normally am able to put on a brave face amidst my pain, but this was not a pain I could brave. It was beyond my coping skills.

This pain- no, this storm- needed more than just me. It needed Jesus and my family's grace.

This bully needed to have a "come-to-Jesus meeting", and all I could do was pray, trust, and heal; while I rested in the truth that I wasn't alone. These are the moments we are in the belly of the boat with Jesus. Snuggled up next to Him. Trusting. We can't row. We can't raise a sail. We feel useless. We can only rest and raise a prayer. And it's in our trusting rest that we get glimpses of the storm walker.

I truly hope I am not babbling here, and you are able to see my connections I am attempting to make.

Storms that the enemy sends to bully us, Jesus sends *us* to confront. You and me!

While my family confronted the caregiving storm, I confronted the tormenting one. While my family warred for my healing, I had to rest in *my pause*.

My health crisis created my own storm and in turn, developed a typhoon for my family to sail through. And where would I be if they didn't?

I am still recovering from that storm because it had created a chain reaction in my body. And although I still have health issues, I am not suffering in hopelessness.

There will be times that God calls you away from the crowd. He may call you away from your ministry or your circle of influence, and ask you to step in the boat, and be willing to go through the flesh ripping storm for *one* soul.

He may ask you to tread on the devil's porch, even if your knees are knocking and you're about to face something that terrifies you. A storm so big, that even with Jesus PHYSICALLY in the boat, fear still tries to rise up in you.
You must withstand the storm!

And beware, some storms may cause you to struggle with thoughts that you may have missed hearing God properly. The pelting rain causes you to lose sight of Jesus in the boat. You will wonder what is so valuable on the other side of the sea that you have to endure a hurricane

You will wrestle with the idea of leaving a cheering crowd behind. You will wonder, "If I was obeying God, why am I going through so much suffering?"

Destiny-stopping storms can make us want to row the boat back to the shore.

Fear may be looming, and you may already be weary from war, but you must keep mustering your mustard seed faith, and get in the boat!

There is purpose, victory and a new level of anointing waiting for you on the other side of the storm.

GRIEF

"No one ever told me that grief felt so like fear" – *C.S. Lewis*

I want to briefly touch on the bully of Grief and how it can torment us with fear. Grief is part of life, but the *spirit* of grief is not.

Grief can come in different ways, but for some, the deepest one is death. It's like living with an amputation. Somebody who you loved deeply is gone and now you need to learn to live without them.

If they were a big presence in your life, then there will be a big empty place. And, oh man, can that emptiness bully you. If you don't lift your eyes and see hope and life beyond your grief, you may stay camped in your Death Valley.

I've buried a few loved ones in my life, and for me, the first year of their absence wasn't the worst. It was the second and third. Maybe it's because my children serve in the military and I am used to not seeing loved ones faces for a year or so.

But time ticks away and the bubble of the first year pops, and then the journey of living without someone really begins; another birthday, another Christmas, another mile marker of their empty chair at the table.

I'm reminded of Naomi in the book of Ruth. Naomi was full of faith and hope, awe and wonder. She was full of new possibilities that filled her heart when her family moved to new territory.

Her boys got married and life was full of opportunities. But the swing of the ugly arm of death cleared the table and took her husband and two boys from their seats. She looked around at the rubble and scratched her head, and thought, "wow, that didn't go as planned."

But the grief storm that tried to destroy her, only detoured her.

She lifted her eyes. She refused to stay bowed down to the spirit of grief, and she packed her bags and left it behind.

I'm sure you can understand how difficult that must have been for Naomi. She left the graves of her family, her beloved husband, her precious boys, and moved back to her hometown.

I've read stories about women on the Oregon Trail who lost their children to sickness or disease. The anguish they went through, because they had to pioneer on and leave the graves of their babies behind, was pure torture.

They would need to make sure their graves were deep to keep wild animals from digging up their children. And then, they had to keep on trucking because they were not yet where they set out to be. Grief stricken and an empty place in the carriage, these courageous women pioneered on for the future of those who were still in the wagon!

However, even in Naomi's heaviness, she carried others to where they needed to be. Ruth reaped the benefits of Naomi being fearless and making a move in her grief. We know how this story ends. Because of Naomi, Ruth is grafted into the lineage of Jesus.

Naomi's rode the waves of her death storm to new beginnings. She opened doors for others, and in doing so, became the great, great, great, (you get my point) great grandma of Jesus!

She is an incredible example of a woman withstanding a storm and being the one to rescue others.

DEPRESSION

"Although the world is full of suffering, it is also full of overcoming it." -Helen Keller

The Hebrew meaning for depression is misery and trouble. It comes from the root word, browbeating. Sheesh, ain't that the truth? I could camp out on this subject all day and how we should confront it.

But, I did say this was a little book, so I will stick to my guns. I just want to quickly touch on it for now.

There are countless people in the Bible who struggled with depression and found ways to overcome. People like David, Elijah, Job, and Hannah.

Depression is different than sadness. It's a feeling of weariness, grief, and isolation. And sleep does not help when the soul is tired.

We will have moments, days, weeks, or even seasons of depression. The weather, our health, relationship troubles, a hurting child, a broken friendship, finances, marriage problems, and a death, can slip us into depression.

And I know memories, traumas, and failures can sink us into a place of despair as well. Giving us a feeling of no way out of the movie that reminds us of the pain.

Depression likes to come in and make itself at home in our heart and kick out all the other residents, like joy, laughter, silliness, fun, and adventure.

My way to combat this bully is to invite all those wonderful things into my life and kick it up the notch. I surround myself with articles that bring me joy. They may not make sense to some, but it is my arsenal against this oppressing bully.

It could be a color, a picture, a saying, or even a project. If it makes me smile and brings delight, I will buy it or find a way to bring it into my home.

During the worst part of my illness, I hung up yellow curtains all throughout my living room. We painted our kitchen in happy new colors. I brought light into my house in any way I could. Christmas lights in my hutch and twinkle lights in little jars.

God would give me words to declare and I would find those words on plaques or letters and hang them on my walls. Or, if I couldn't find them already made, I'd give Joe the fun job of making them for me. My children say our home looks like Hobby Lobby with all my pictures and quotes. I'll take that as a compliment

I refused to let misery reside in my heart and home. This bully would not be a regular guest. This hateful harasser likes to own the room. He pulls our faces down and our eyes low.

There were times I had to prop my face up on all my faith and positive quotes to see Jesus.

It's an unavoidable fact that you will have sad days. You will have sorrow and you will have depressed moods (also known as hormones at times), but it doesn't have to be a lifestyle.

I am very aware people need to see doctors or counselors or therapists or take medication and that is okay. That is called combatting! When you are seeking help, you are fighting off the enemy and you are strategizing.

Do not let anyone shame you for needing help! It is courageous to seek help and solutions. You go girl!

It's when we stop fighting and relinquish our joy to the enemy, that this monster changes our life and rearranges the furniture. Never stop getting back up after a bout with depression. Fight the good fight! Hold fast! Don't shrink back!

"Courage doesn't always roar. Sometimes courage is the little voice at the end of the day that says, I'll try again tomorrow"
-Mary Ann Radmacher

Anxiety in the heart of man causes depression, but a good word makes it glad. Proverbs 12:25 NKJV

When I said, "my foot is slipping," your unfailing love, Lord, supported me. When anxiety was great within me, your consolation brought me joy. Psalms 94: 18,19 NIV

INSECURITIES

Confidence is not, 'They'll like me.' Confidence is, 'I'll be fine if they don't'" -Christina Grimmie

Judges 6:1-13 describes the perfect moment of shrinking back due to fear and oppression. The harassment of the enemy caused a man named Gideon to become a cave dweller; threshing wheat in a wine press. In today's day and age, we would be held up in our homes watching Netflix or Disney Plus and avoiding people.

I find it interesting that Gideon is in a cave threshing wheat. Back then, they needed wind to thresh wheat correctly. However, ol' Gid was trying to use equipment that was meant for pressing and refining and aging. But what was required to get the job done was a nice breeze or a gust of wind: The Breath of God.

Due to the abuse of the enemy, Gideon was pushed back to a stale cave, void of light and fresh air; a place that smelled of old wineskins.

He was doing a job he wasn't made for and with the wrong tools, becoming smaller and smaller and smaller with every step into the cave. There was a fighter somewhere in this bat cave, but it took an outside voice to call it forth.

The angel of the Lord appeared to him and said, "Mighty hero, the Lord is with you!" Judges 6:12 NLT

The last thing we feel like when we are in hiding, is a hero. And Gideon knows full and well he is reduced to a cave dwelling coward. But, GOD! God saw the hero in him. He saw that Gideon would rise to the challenge even if he was hiding, afraid, weak, and insecure.

Then the Lord turned to him and said, "Go with the strength you have, and rescue Israel from the Midianites. I am sending you!"
Judges 6:14 NLT

We all need an Alfred to remind us we're Batman. We need someone who sees the giant slayer and remembers who we are when we forget. Like verse 12 declares, *"Mighty hero, the Lord is with you!"*

And when we don't need an Alfred, we need to be an Alfred for someone else. We must watch out for our friends, our sisters, children and grandchild, those we fellowship with. We need to be vigilant in our love and care for them. And if they need someone to remind them they are a warrior or a hero, then be that person.

When I was younger, I battled with self-worth. I knew I was loved by my family. But I felt average in every way. The only thing that would stand out about me was my messy hair, my clumsiness, and my awkward sense of humor.

In grade school these things got me teased. In Junior High, these delightful insecurities got highlighted with pimples, armpit hair, and training bras.

But then High School came; boobs were good. Wild hair was cool (It was the 80's), and my silly personality somehow became accepted.

You see, history will always try to tell us what is acceptable. And, God forbid, you go against the media's idea of beauty or size.

Unafraid

I read an article about Gillet razors. In the 50's Gillet created an ad campaign targeted towards women and their armpit hair? In fact, the slogan was, "no more ugly armpit hair".

It wasn't a common practice to shave your armpits, but Gillet wanted to sell more products, so they created an insecurity to market to; then they offered the solution. Women's razors and shaving cream.

If this doesn't chap your khakis, I don't know what will. Girls, we are being targeted to hate ourselves. We are being marketed to despise our body, hair, face; and for what? A style? A decade fad? Corporate greed?

Next year big hips may be in, and the thinner the lips the better. Who knows? I am holding out for this fashion because when it comes into style, I am the Cover Girl!

THE PAUSE

"Never underestimate what God is doing during your season of waiting"-me, I said that

"While you're waiting. God is working."
-Rick Warren

Now, I realize there will be times when we need to step away. But do not confuse stepping away with running away.

There are going to be periods and seasons in our life where the only thing we can do, and must do, is heal.

And that, in itself, is enough. It takes courage to sit out for a while to recover. But in that time of healing and regaining our strength, we must guard our hearts with all diligence to make sure we are not going backwards.

Being on pause is fine. It's a vacation house, an Airbnb, or a timeshare, but it is not a thirty year mortgage.

The most important thing we can do during our times of pause, is to be restful and watchful.

This is the time the enemy wants to come in and set us back and surround us with a hopelessness that can feel engulfing. He craves to take what territory we have gained. His desire is to torment us, cause us to feel doubt of our purpose and discourage us in our waiting. He wants us to be fearful of trying again, fearful of failure, fearful of looking foolish, to be fearful of dreaming again, and fearful of hoping again.

We can't let a pause cause us to shrink back. Pauses are not punishment!!!!! I repeat, a pause is not punishment!!!!!

It is not a *time-out* for bad behavior. You're not in the penalty box. It is a reprieve. It's a time of refreshing and a time to be lavished by the Father.

So, stay faithful in prayer, diligent in the Word, and accountable with your walk.

A pause is where the enemy loves to ensnare us. He loves to have us falter in times of trouble, shrink our faith, and cause us to forget our purpose and become bitter, bored, or broken.

Whatever tactic works, he doesn't care. If we believe the lie that God has forgotten us, then we have let the enemy triumph.

Don't fear "The Pause" but don't rush it either.

Like all great things, the pause is one of God's favorite ways to grow, mature, and to empower us. A greater anointing waits on the other side of a pause. Why…? (long pause) because a pause brings a dramatic effect!

Let's go back to my buddy Gid. In Judges 6:14, God commands Gideon "To go in the strength you have."

This is a no-nonsense command. It's not asking you to be anything but your authentic self; knowing your strength and your weakness and moving forward in that knowledge.

Our biggest battles happen between our ears. We are most certain of the things we can't do, but seldom focus on what we *can* do.

This moment, right here, in the cave of stale and stinky air, the Breath of God blows the chaff away of Gideon's self-doubt, insecurities, and his waiting period. Sending him to battle with the little he has; because little is much in the hands of God.

"Overcoming your fear is embracing your identity as a son or daughter in Christ."
-Cody Ruddock

God loves to bring increase to the little things. In the moments we are waiting and being still, we must war against the emotion of feeling small, displaced or forgotten during our season of pause.

I am very familiar with the *Pause*. There were times during my life it would look like I was gaining momentum in life or ministry, then something would happen that would sideline me. And though each circumstance needed my full attention, (family crisis, financial disaster, injured child, health emergency) it took me out of the race for a while.

During that time period (nearly ten years) I had to fight the lie that God had forgotten me; that He was done with me and my call as a writer, teacher and speaker. Oh But GOD!!!!!

He loves thundering out of dark places, forgotten places, valleys and deserts of deceased desires and dead dreams. He is passionate about taking the trembling ones and making them stand tall. He relishes in the weak becoming strong, the fearful becoming brave, the broken becoming whole and the *forgotten* becoming known, dry bones revived to life!

Then he said to me, "Speak a prophetic message to these bones and say, 'Dry bones, listen to the word of the Lord! This is what the Sovereign Lord says: Look! I am going to put breath into you and make you live again!'" Ezekiel 37:4-5 NLT

I love that verse. What would our life look like if we took God at His word?

God does not waste our waiting. Our faith is like a bulb planted in the fall for spring blooms. And though it must endure months of dark and cold, it was planted with an intended season of purpose. The frigid nights and the gray days are not forever, dear hearts. Hang on to the truth. You may not hear Him like you want to, or it might even feel that you can't hear Him at all; but do not concede to winters darkness. You will flourish again. Do not let today's circumstance talk you out of what you know is true.

One of my most favorite scenes in a movie is in The Chronicles of Narnia: Prince Caspian. Lucy knows she's seen Aslan, but the others hadn't, so she begins to doubt if she actually sighted him.

But when troubles come, the siblings send Lucy back to where she last saw Aslan. You know what this says to me? They did have some belief in her, but their skepticism cast doubt in Lucy's heart and she came into agreement with the disbelief.

This should be an eye opener for us. We cannot throw away our confidence because of someone's doubt and disbelief.

But then, the siblings needed Lucy's connection and faith she had with Aslan. Therefore, they sent her to the place she saw him last.

Their greeting was warm, and Lucy was excited because she *knew* she *had* seen him. But when Aslan asked her, "Why didn't you come to me?" her answer was filled with regret, "because the others didn't believe me." They thought if he *was* there, then why didn't they see him as well?

Isn't this what we face at times when we try to describe our faith to someone or explain what we are believing God for; to heal, rescue, deliver or provide.

Someone else's doubt should not influence our faith! Our faith should invade their doubt! Stay confident friends. Do not shrink back because of another's disbelief. Get bolder, braver, fiercer!

As the story continues, Aslan and Lucy go and confront an army that is coming to destroy the Narnians. Lucy's only weapon she is carrying is a tiny dagger. Aslan and Lucy with her dagger, was all that was needed to defeat an army.

Every time I see that scene, I think of moments I have felt small. Maybe others doubted me, my gifts, my ability, or my faith, but then I feel the mane of the Lion. I hear His low growl. I sense His presence and know I am not alone. Jesus and I, we are an army.

I love Lucy and her faith.

You, Jesus, and the strength you have, is all you need to win the war against hopelessness, fear, and insecurities; just to name a few storms.

Scripture hidden in your heart is like a dagger hidden in your boot. If the Word of God is a sword, then a memorized verse is a secret weapon in your hand. The enemy doesn't see it coming.

Give God what you have friends. Be unafraid in your surrender. Be courageous in your identity. Be valiant in your pause. Be bold in your change. Be heroic in your newness. Be fearless in your storm.

Get out of that cave, oh, mighty woman of God. Ignored anxiety is not surrendered anxiety, it is suppressed.

Confront what makes you anxious, nervous, timid. You can't change it if you won't confront it. Get in the boat. Face the raging winds. Somebody needs you to weather the storm. Somebody needs you to leave the crowd behind, face your fears, and embrace your new normal.

YOU ARE FEARLESS!

I am going to end with this story;

When I was 12 years old I went on a school trip to Great America. I rode all the safe rides; the kiddie rides, the boring rides, the log ride, the carousel, the octopus, everything that DIDN'T go upside-down or loop-de-loop.

Oh, I wanted to, but I was extremely afraid. I walked by this new ride that I had an especially strong pull towards. It looked quite dangerous with several loop-de-loops, upside-down and twisty-turnies, and I wanted to ride it.

The ride's name was "The Demon". I needed to saddle up and conquer that baby. My dad saw my intrigue toward this perilous ride and as our day was coming to an end, we walked by it one more time.

He said to me, "do you want daddy to go with you?" I said "yes", but controlled my excitement, you know, just in case I changed my mind. Enthusiasm could possibly commit me, and I wanted options to get out of it.

I was thrilled he offered, but I kept it on the low-low. We got in the line, and when it was time to get in our cart my stomach was doing flips! I still had time to back out, I wasn't strapped in, I could run, my exit was close. No one would know that I chickened out, except the few hundred people watching me.

My dad got in first, then motioned for me to sit down next to him. We buckled in and got situated. "The ride still hasn't launched yet, others are still loading, I still have time to bolt," I thought.

He interrupts my panicky thoughts with the question, "do you want to hold my hand?" He holds out his rough, giant hand and I grab it with all my twelve-year old strength. And the ride takes off!

Upside-down, up, over, loop-de-loops, and twisty-turnies. My head flung from side-to-side and I was tossed around like a rag doll, and IT WAS MARVELOUS! We disembarked and I was absolutely elated. It was the best time I had since we got there.

What was I so afraid of? It was the upside-down part; I had never done that before. I had passed the test and I was now an official big-kid-roller-coaster rider. No more baby rides for me.

My father not only helped me face The Demon, he gave me courage to get in line and go again. This time I took the bravery my dad imparted to me and rode The Demon alone. I realized it couldn't hurt me, just scare me.

By the way, my dad's life scripture was Joshua 1:9 - *This is my command — be strong and courageous! Do not be afraid or discouraged. For the LORD your God is with you wherever you go.*

He lived this out loud and I desire to follow in my father's footsteps.

Sisters, be courageous on your roller coaster. Stand up to the bully of lies, depression, grief, and insecurities. Face the demon of fear.

Confront what has you cornered in a cave. You were created to WIN! You were crafted to rise up and *be the storm* in the enemies life!

You have the DNA of an overcomer, victorious, resurrected God. You were shaped from winning material and are fashioned for facing hard things.

You were created to rise from the ashes of defeat and be a conquer. So straighten your crown, fluff that toto, roll those sleeves up and live UNAFRAID

Unafraid

A Few Scriptures To Be Unafraid

"Are you tired? Worn out? Burned out on religion? Come to me. Get away with me and you'll recover your life. I'll show you how to take a real rest. Walk with me and work with me – watch how I do it. Learn the unforced rhythms of grace. I won't lay anything heavy or ill-fitting on you. Keep company with me and you'll learn to live freely and lightly." (Matthew 11:28-30 MSG)

Don't worry about anything; instead, pray about everything. Tell God what you need and thank him for all he has done. Then you will experience God's peace, which exceeds anything we can understand. His peace will guard your hearts and minds as you live in Christ Jesus. And now, dear brothers and sisters, one final thing. Fix your thoughts on what is true, and honorable, and right, and pure, and

Unafraid

lovely, and admirable. Think about things that are excellent and worthy of praise. Keep putting into practice all you learned and received from me — everything you heard from me and saw me doing. Then the God of peace will be with you.
Philippians 4:6-9 NLT

Cast all your anxiety on him because he cares for you. (1 Peter 5:7 NIV)

Who stood up for me against the wicked? Who took my side against evil workers? If God hadn't been there for me, I never would have made it. The minute I said, "I'm slipping, I'm falling," your love, God, took hold and held me fast. When I was upset and beside myself, you calmed me down and cheered me up. (Psalm 94:16-19 MSG)

When anxiety was great within me, your consolation brought me joy. (Psalm 94:19 NIV)

God met me more than halfway, he freed me from my anxious fears. (Psalm 34:4 MSG)

..., for we have the mind of Christ. (1 Corinthians 2:16

...Don't be dejected and sad, for the joy of the Lord is your strength!" (Nehemiah 8:10 NLT)

There is no fear in love. But perfect love drives out fear... John 4:18 NIV)

I sought the Lord, and he answered me; he delivered me from all my fears. Those who look to him are radiant; their faces are never covered with shame. (Psalm 34:4, 5 NIV)

For God has not given us a spirit of fear, but of power and of love and of a sound mind. (2 Timothy 1:7 NKJV)

You, dear children, are from God and have overcome them, because the one who is in you is greater than the one who is in the world. (1 John 4:4 NIV)

They triumphed over him by the blood of the Lamb and by the word of their testimony; they did not love their lives so much as to shrink from death. (Revelation 12:11 NIV)

For I know the plans I have for you," declares the Lord, "plans to prosper you and not to harm you, plans to give you hope and a future. (Jeremiah 29:11 NIV)

"Here's what I want you to do: Find a quiet, secluded place so you won't be tempted to role-play before God. Just be there as simply and honestly as you can manage. The focus will shift from you to God, and you will begin to sense his grace. (Matthew 6:6 MSG)

Unafraid

Holly Ruddock could be described as; Passionate, down-to-earth, relatable and witty.

As an author, blogger, bible study teacher and speaker, Holly transparently shares her life story. Weaving the word of God with personal experiences, she will make you laugh, cry and possibly snort. She open shares overcoming insecurities and learning to take God at His word over her life.

As a mother to four military children, she will often speak of the joys and anxiety that comes with being a mom to four heroes. You will frequently find her encouraging and mentoring military families to anchor deep and hold fast to God's promises, by declaring the word of God over our children's lives. Learning to trust Father God with our kids when they choose a life of sacrifice, means to understand the omnipresence of Jesus in a whole new level. She will say things like "trusting in the scary moments is not the changing of the guards." What she means by that, is that our trust needs to be just as great and courageous when our children are in our care and when they are out of our sight. It is an understanding that the God of angel armies goes into places we could never get to.

In her victories, failures, flops and all the in-betweens, Holly draws you in with her storytelling ways, backing up her experience and inspirational thoughts with God's Word. She will challenge you to dream and dare you to hope.

Her heart breaks over the injustices she sees in our broken world, and longs to bring change with small acts of obedience and generous acts of love.

When she is not writing or teaching she loves to find healthy new recipes to "pin" and new coffee shops to explore. One of her great delights is taking adventurers in her lime green, 76 VW bus with her high school sweetheart and husband of thirty-two years Joe. They live on the beautiful Kitsap Peninsula and love gardening together and trying sipping java juice and trying hole in the wall restaurants. She relishes time spent with her husband and her four military children and grandbabies and she will stop her world to spend as much time with them around the family firepit.

Made in the USA
Coppell, TX
13 March 2021